Squirrel Coloring Book

Get FREE printable coloring pages and discounted book prices sent straight to your e-mail inbox every week!

Sign up at:

www.adultcoloringworld.net

ISBN-13: 978-1530587056
ISBN-10: 1530587050

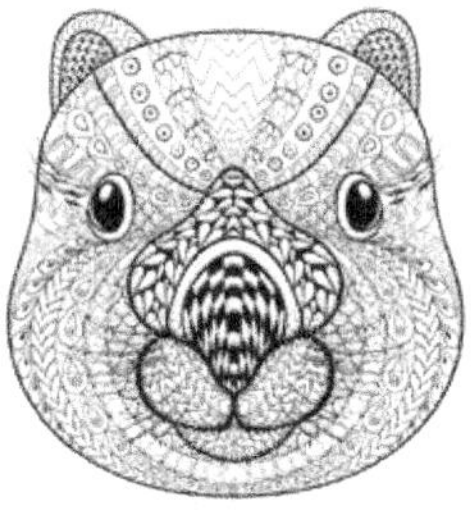

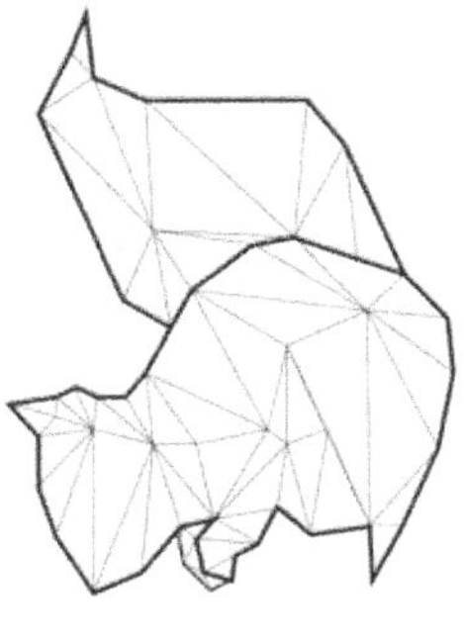

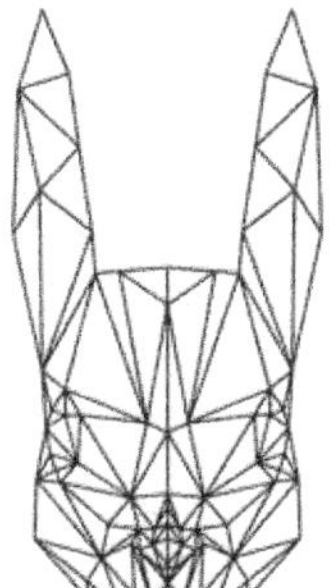

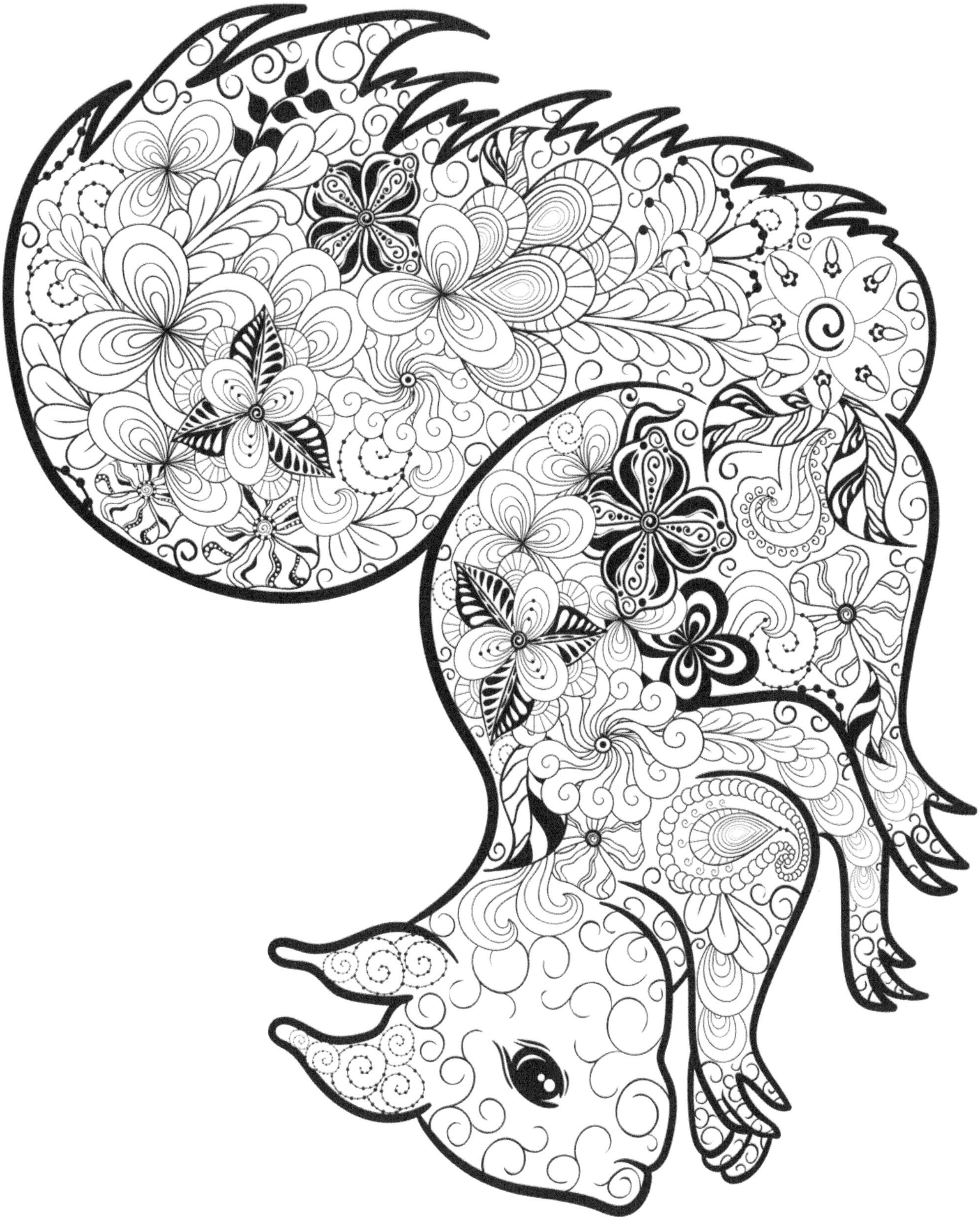

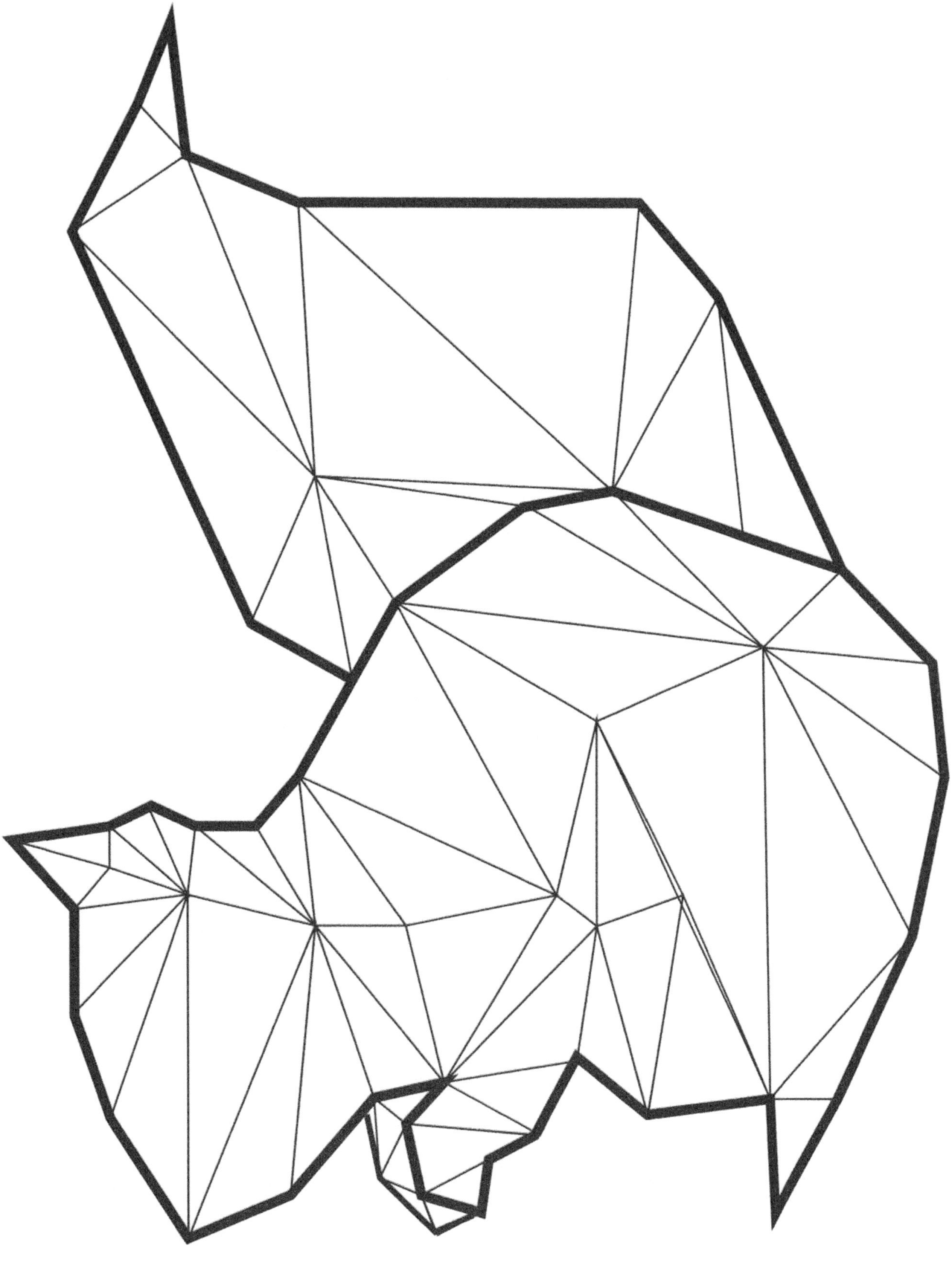

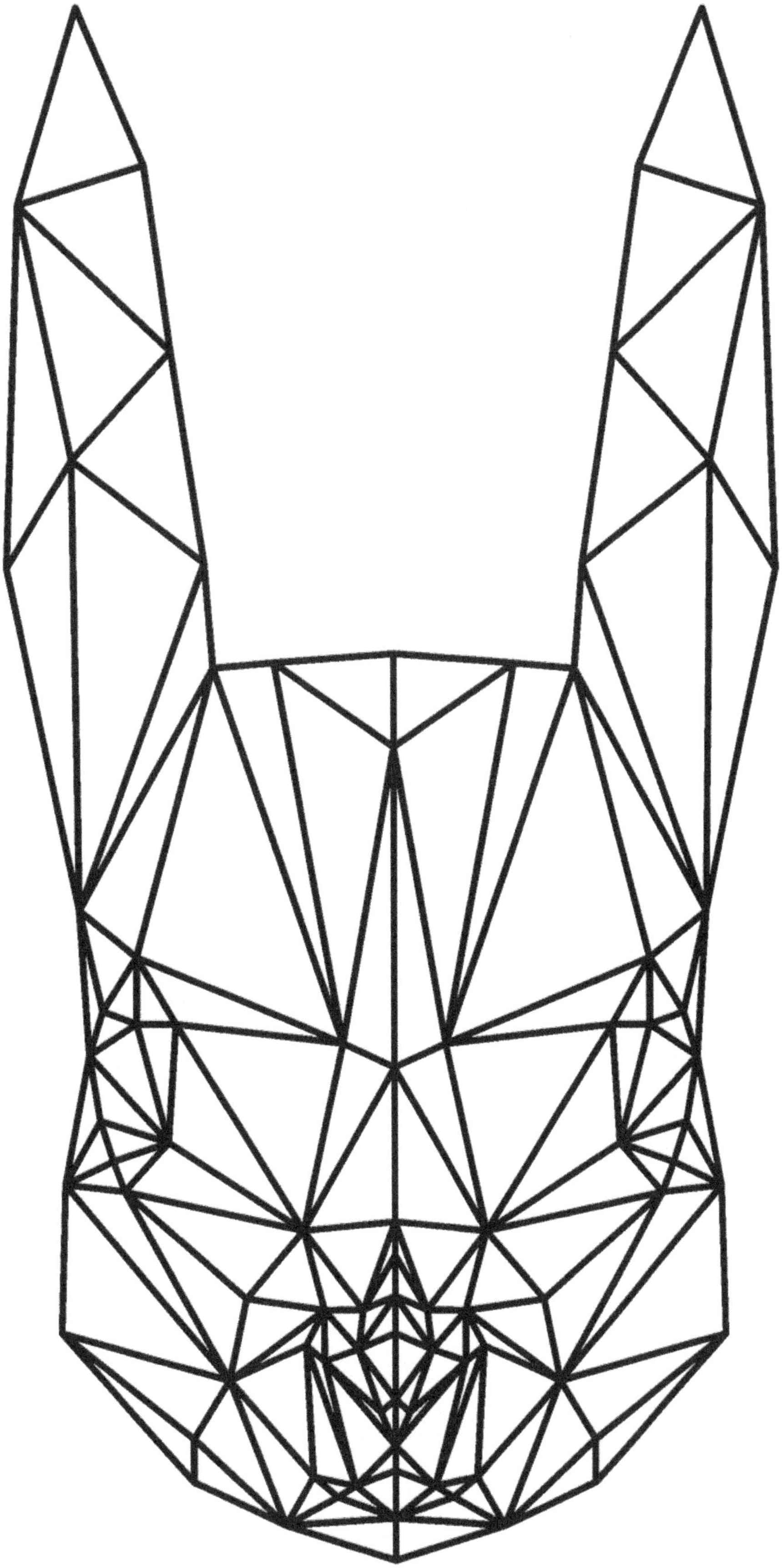

Color Test Page

Color Test Page

Made in the USA
Monee, IL
20 December 2019

19312131R00031